LINCOLNWOOD PUBLIC LIBRARY
W9-BMQ-194

BISON
IVING WILD

LIVING WILD

Published by Creative Education
P.O. Box 227, Mankato, Minnesota 56002
Creative Education is an imprint of The Creative Company
www.thecreativecompany.us

Design and production by Mary Herrmann
Art direction by Rita Marshall
Printed by Corporate Graphics in the United States of America

Photographs by Alamy (All Canada Photos, Alex Hibbert, Photo Network), Corbis (Werner Forman, Layne Kennedy), Dreamstime (Alain, James Cottingham, Tom Dowd, Dssimages, Jkfyates, Karis2, Steve Keller, Lehmanphotos, Mike Norton, Mark Rasmussen, Mike Rogal, Tdmartin, Vanessagifford, Vchphoto, Vasiliy Vishnevskiy), Getty Images (Buyenlarge, Frank Krahmer, David McNew, Charles Marion Russell), iStockphoto (Jorge Delgado, Eric Foltz, Roy Marx, Conor Quinlan), Shutterstock (Claudia Holzmann)

Library of Congress Cataloging-in-Publication Data
Gish, Melissa.
Bison / by Melissa Gish.
p. cm. — (Living wild)
Includes bibliographical references and index.
Summary: A look at bison, including their habitats, physical characteristics such as their shaggy coats, behaviors, relationships with humans, and threatened status in the world today.
ISBN 978-1-60818-077-6
1. American bison—Juvenile literature. I. Title.

QL737.U53G57 2011
599.64'3—dc22 2010028305

CPSIA: 110310 PO1385

First Edition
9 8 7 6 5 4 3 2 1

CREATIVE EDUCATION

BISON

Melissa Gish

On the plains of Yellowstone National Park,

a soft summer breeze

rustles through dense blue grama grass.

On the plains of Yellowstone National Park, a soft summer breeze rustles through dense blue grama grass. A band of 20 American bison—females and juveniles, all led by a dominant male—stand as still as statues, except for the slow motion of their jaws as they casually chew. One of the juvenile males ambles away from the group, moving toward a shallow depression in the ground—covering nearly 200 square feet (18.6 sq m)—where the earth is bare.

He throws himself into the depression, called a wallow, and kicks his feet toward the sky, twisting and rolling around in the dust. Grunting and kicking, the bison packs his fur full of cool earth. After several minutes, the young bison clambers back to his feet. He moves toward the band, dirt falling from his coat with every step. The fine dust packed into his fur will keep him comfortable for the remainder of the afternoon.

WHERE IN THE WORLD THEY LIVE

Plains Bison southern Canada, west and central United States

Wood Bison northern Canada and Alaska

European Bison eastern Europe

The two subspecies of American bison, plains and wood bison, live in the mid- and northwestern United States and Canada, with the largest population of plains bison residing in Yellowstone National Park, and wood bison living on preserves in northern Canada and being reintroduced to native grounds in Alaska. European bison (also known as wisent) inhabit parts of eastern European countries such as Poland and Belarus. The colored squares represent some of the areas in which wild bison are found today.

The American bison is 1 of the 140 members of the Bovidae family, which is made up of cloven-hoofed, hollow-horned animals. Also called "buffalo" (despite its not being a true buffalo), the bison is the largest land animal in North America. It is the second-largest hoofed animal in the world after its Asian relative, the gaur. Bison have many relatives—from the African buffalo and numerous species of antelope, gazelle, and goat, to the common cow, which is its closest relation. The earliest ancestors of bovids **evolved** almost 20 million years ago in southern Asia. Today, bovids are found all across Europe, Africa, Asia, and North America.

Scientists split the American bison into two subspecies: wood bison of northern Canada and plains bison of southern Canada and the central and western U.S. A similar species, the European bison of eastern Europe—known as the wisent (*VY-zent*)—is shorter but heavier than the American bison. The International Union for Conservation of Nature (IUCN) lists the wisent as a vulnerable species, which means it is likely to become

The largest populations of gaur (GOW-er) are found in India, where this animal is also known as the Indian bison.

Today's wild American bison are descended from 88 captured bison and the last 23 bison from a Yellowstone herd in the 1870s.

endangered in the future unless changes are made to improve its chances of survival. *Bison* is a Latin word meaning "wild ox" that was first used to describe the wisent. In the late 17th century, European explorers used the same word to describe the North American variety of these shaggy, horned animals.

Like all bovids, bison have horns. The horns of both male and female bison are permanently attached to their skulls. Unlike the antlers of deer and moose, which are shed seasonally, bison horns never fall off unless they are broken off, and they continue to grow throughout the animal's life. The horns are made of bone covered with a layer of keratin—the same substance that is found in human fingernails. There is an air pocket between the bone and the keratin, though, which is why bovids are known as hollow-horned animals.

Bison and their relatives are mammals. All mammals, with the exceptions of the platypus and hedgehog-like echidna, give birth to live offspring and produce milk to feed their young. Mammals are warm-blooded animals. This means that they are able to keep their body temperature at a constant level, no matter what the

Unlike American bison (pictured), which vocalize extensively, the wisent makes only abrupt snorts or grunts.

Grass loses some of its nutrients when it dries, but bison have adapted to require fewer nutrients in winter than in summer.

temperature is outside. Bison have a thick, curly coat of **insulating** fur that helps keep them warm and varies from dark brown to black in color. Males have a thick mane of darker fur around their shoulders and neck.

In winter, bison grow a second layer of fur to keep them warm in their cold, northern habitats. Close to the body is a coat of thick, curly underfur that traps heat close to the skin. On top of the underfur are long guard hairs. These hairs are thick and oily, enabling snow and rain to slide off the bison. The winter fur on a bison's hindquarters can grow to be 8 inches (20.3 cm) long, and the fur on its forelegs can reach 10 inches (25.4 cm) in length. The curly mop of fur on a bison's forehead can measure up to 16 inches (41 cm) in length. Both males and females have a beard that hangs beneath the chin.

American bison have a unique characteristic—the large hump on their shoulders, which is composed of muscles that are supported by extra-long spinal bones. A higher, squarer shoulder hump makes the wood bison appear taller than the plains bison, and while both subspecies average 12.5 feet (3.8 m) in length, the wood bison typically weighs about 15 percent more than the

Bison can produce enough body heat to keep them warm at all times, which allows only bison (not cattle) to winter in frozen pastures.

Stampeding bison will blindly follow their herd leader, stopping only when the leader comes to a halt.

plains bison. Plains bison can weigh up to 1,800 pounds (817 kg), and wood bison can reach 2,250 pounds (1,021 kg). Males, called bulls, stand about 6.5 feet (2 m) tall at the shoulder, while females, called cows, are somewhat smaller. A bison's weight **fluctuates** with the seasons, as the animal adds bulk in summer when food is plentiful and loses weight in winter when less food is needed.

Despite this massive size, bison can move quickly on land and are able to run at speeds of up to 35 miles (56 km) per hour in short bursts. They are also agile and can turn sharply while running. They have excellent hearing and an acute sense of smell that enables them to detect other animals from nearly two miles (3.2 km) away. Bison have poor eyesight, however, and are unable to see clearly from a distance, which makes their behavior unpredictable and therefore potentially dangerous. Their body language may offer some clue as to their mood and whether they intend to move or not. A loosely hanging tail indicates relaxation, a stiff horizontal tail shows excitement, and an upward-pointing tail means a bison is angry and ready to charge. Bison may charge any object—from other animals to people in vehicles—not to fight, but to protect themselves or their young.

Yellowstone National Park is home to the world's largest free-roaming bison population—about 4,000 individuals in numerous herds.

Bison use their hooves and horns to dig as deep as four feet (1.2 m) into winter snow to uncover still-green grasses.

Bison have strong neck and shoulder muscles that they use to swing their heads—which can weigh from 50 to 75 pounds (23–34 kg)—from side to side to clear deep snow from the ground like a snowplow. On the prairie, bison use their hooves to dig out grass and form wallows. These depressions can be up to 14 feet (4.3 m) across and 1 foot (30.5 cm) deep. Bison roll around in the wallows, coating their fur with dust or mud to cool off or as protection from biting insects. In spring, bison may roll furiously in the wallows to loosen their winter fur. They also rub against rocks and trees to help shed winter coats.

Bison have a special stomach—one with four chambers, or sections—that allows them to eat woody food such as twigs and bark, which most other animals find indigestible. Food passes through the first chamber, called the rumen, where bacteria and acids soften it. Then the food is regurgitated, or brought back up to the mouth. This food mass, called a cud, is chewed again. When it is swallowed, the cud passes through all four stomach chambers to be fully digested. Bison share this trait of cud chewing with cows, sheep, giraffes, llamas, moose, and many other hoofed mammals classified as ruminants.

The hair on a bison's forehead can be 16 inches (41 cm) long, while it is only half that length on the hindquarters.

Fighting males may crash headfirst into each other up to 20 times before one animal tires and backs down.

ON THE OPEN PRAIRIE

Bison are social animals, and for most of the year they live in groups called bands. Made up of either all adult males or all adult females and their offspring, a band may contain up to 60 members. A dominant male or female leads each band. Although they are usually separate, bands often gather close together, with each staying within established territories. This larger collective, called a herd, may number in the thousands and is typically led by an older cow. Bison communicate with other members of the herd by grunting periodically. Males may bellow aggressively when challenging each other for grazing area. The magnitude of the bellow signals the animal's strength, so one bull usually backs out of the challenge before physical contact occurs.

Herds move from place to place as they graze, usually traveling an average of three miles (4.8 km) per day from where they started. Because they need to drink water almost every day, bison will follow established trails to water sources. In winter, they eat snow or break through the ice covering puddles and streams. Bison are strong swimmers and can cross fast-moving rivers.

Since 23 plains bison were first relocated to Fairbanks, Alaska, in 1928, the herd has grown to nearly 500 individuals.

Bison play a vital balancing role in the **food chains** of their habitats, preventing overgrowth of grasslands by eating selectively in large areas. They are vegetarians—feeding on grasses, mosses, twigs, bark, and occasional berries—and must continually forage for food, even in winter. Bison eat less food in winter than in summer, not necessarily because food is scarce but because the animals group together to conserve heat, and their body systems slow down to save energy. They need less food because they use less energy. Bison follow a fairly regular daily schedule of eating, regurgitating, and chewing their cud.

As bison graze in summer, the herd moves from place to place, feeding on a variety of grasses and sedges. They may also eat **lichens** (*LY-kenz*), which grow on rocks, trees, and hard-packed soil surfaces. Lichens grow even in the coldest climates, which makes them an ideal food source for bison during the winter.

Experts advise bison observers to remain at least 300 feet (91.4 m) away from the herd for safety's sake.

Wood bison remain in their forests year round. Plains bison typically leave the open prairie in winter, migrating to wooded areas for shelter and winter food sources. The herd gathers closer together as the animals seek warmth and safety from their main predators: wolves and bears.

A bison cow can live to be 25 years old in the wild and, upon maturity, is capable of giving birth once every year.

These animals typically do not attack bull bison, choosing instead to prey on weak, injured, or old bison, as well as the young. A bear bites the bison's throat to cut off its air supply and then devours it. Wolves hunt in groups called packs and bite at the legs and throats of the bison. Biting the legs cripples a bison, sending it tumbling to the ground, where the wolf pack can pounce on it. A bison's best defense is to run away from predators. It can outrun bears but not always wolves. Bison will use their hooves and horns as weapons when cornered.

Toward the end of winter, plains bison move back onto the open prairie, drifting apart into their bands once again. From June to September, it is mating season for American bison. Female bison are ready to mate when they are two to three years old. Males do not mature until they are about six years old. During mating season, males that are ready to mate move into territories occupied by female bands. They dig wallows and roll around in them, leaving scent marks as displays of strength designed to attract females. A bull will then select a cow and stand between her and the rest of the herd. This behavior is called tending. If a cow is not interested in the bull, she will walk around him and return to the herd. If she does wish to mate with him, she will allow him to tend her.

A male may tend his potential mate for as little as a few minutes to as long as several days. If another male approaches the selected female, her suitor will defend her fiercely. The male will stomp the ground, snort, and charge at intruders. Sometimes fights occur between males competing for females. Bulls may butt heads, shove each other, or lock horns to try to push each other to the ground. While battles to the death are rare, serious injuries and scars are common.

After a bull mates with one cow, he will leave her and seek other cows with which to mate. After about a nine-and-a-half-month **gestation**, the pregnant female will give birth. Cows usually have just one baby, called a calf, per year, and they rarely give birth to twins. A bison calf is born with its eyes open and weighs anywhere from 30 to 70 pounds (13.6–31.8 kg). It is able to stand within minutes and run after only a few hours. It immediately begins feeding on the milk produced by its mother. A bison calf's reddish-tan coloration helps it blend in with the tall prairie grass for extra safety from predators.

Wolves and bison share a habitat in Yellowstone National Park, but wolves usually hunt elk instead of bison.

European bison have been known to leap over 6-foot-tall (1.8 m) fences and jump across 10-foot-wide (3 m) streams.

Mother bison are fiercely protective and keep their young constantly near them for the first few weeks after birth. Gradually, the calves become more independent and playful, seeking each other out to form collectives called nursery groups. Vigilant mother bison keep on the lookout for predators as the calves romp and chase each other, strengthening their muscles in preparation for the approaching winter and forming bonds that will remain strong in their wintering herd for their entire lives.

Although it begins to eat vegetation in its first month, a calf depends on its mother's nutrient-rich milk until it is 7 months old, when it can weigh more than 400 pounds (181 kg). A calf will remain with its mother through the winter months. During this time, a young bison's fur darkens, and it typically reaches half its adult size. Occasionally, a calf may continue to nurse from its mother for several months afterward, as long as she does not become pregnant again. If its mother does become pregnant again, a young bison will leave her when the new calf is born. Now about two years old, young bulls join all-male bands, and young cows may either remain in their mothers' bands or join different ones.

Bison cows share the responsibility of protecting calves and teaching them how to behave as members of the herd.

FROM "THE BLACKFEET"

I.

Where the snow-world of the mountains
Fronts the sea-like world of sward,
And encamped along the prairies
Tower the white peaks heavenward;
Where they stand by dawn rose-coloured
Or dim-silvered by the stars,
And behind their shadowed portals
Evening draws her lurid bars,
Lies a country whose sweet grasses
Richly clothe the rolling plain;
All its swelling upland pastures
Speak of Plenty's happy reign;
There the bison herds in autumn
Roamed wide sunlit solitudes,
Seamed with many an azure river
Bright in burnished poplar woods.

II.

Night-dews pearled the painted hide-tents,
"Moyas" named, that on the mead
Sheltered dark-eyed women wearing
Braided hair and woven bead.
Never man had seen their lodges,
Never warrior crossed the slopes
Where they rode, and where they hunted
Imu bulls and antelopes.
Masterless, how swift their riding!
While the wild steeds onward flew,
From round breasts and arms unburdened
Freedom's winds their tresses blew.
Only when the purple shadows
Slowly veiled the darkening plain
Would they sorrow that the Sun-god
Dearer loved his Alp's domain.

by John Campbell (1845–1914)

THUNDER ON THE PLAINS

Bison once numbered in the tens of millions and covered the vast grasslands of North America's Great Plains from Canada to Mexico. The area was sometimes called "Buffalo Nation," a place where enormous herds of bison stampeded over rolling, grassy hills, the sounds of their thundering hooves echoing across the land. Settlers crossing the prairies in the early 1800s could hear the bison before they saw them. Unfortunately, within 100 years, this thunder would disappear as the great herds were virtually wiped out by careless overhunting and slaughter for the sake of sport.

Archaeologists know that as far back as 10,000 years before Europeans settled in North America, humans hunted bison to survive. Armed only with small weapons and lacking horses, the earliest people likely drove stampeding bison off cliffs. By the mid-1600s, when horses arrived in North America, hunters could run down individual bison on horseback, shooting them with stone arrowheads. No part of a bison was wasted by these native hunters. Its hide provided clothing and blankets, and its meat was salted and dried into a type of

Between 1830 and 1860, the demand for bison hides and tongues peaked, leading to 200,000 bison being killed each year.

A bison skull often served as the centerpiece in natives' arrangements of sacred objects for use in rituals and ceremonies.

jerky that sustained people through harsh winters. Bison bones were made into tools—everything from sewing needles to hammers. Organs were dried and ground up to make medicine, and even the hooves were cooked into a substance that could be used like glue.

Apart from their practical applications, bison were also valued as sacred objects. Each native tribe had its own ideas about and images of bison. Small bison statues carved from wood were used by spiritual leaders as talismans—objects believed to give magical powers of healing or protection to their bearers—stuffed toys were made of bison fur, and masks and shields bearing images of bison were used in ritual dances. Pipes carved from stone were shaped like bison, and bison skulls were painted for use in sacred ceremonies. While some tribes believed that bison lived in a great underground cavern, and others believed bison lived mysteriously beneath a lake, virtually every Great Plains culture believed in a Great Spirit who sent bison to nourish and protect the people.

Many tribes held ceremonies and dances before a bison hunt to pray for their hunters' safety and success and then afterward to thank the spirits of the bison for their

sacrifice. The medicine man, or priest, in a Cheyenne tribe wore a sacred cap, or *Is'siwun*, made of bison hide and handpainted horns. The Blackfeet prayed using the *Iniskim*, a special stone they believed would draw the bison to their hunting grounds.

Many American Indian tribes saw the bison headdress as a symbol of health and prosperity.

A pair of bronze bison—each 5,000 pounds (2,268 kg)—guards the grand staircase of Winnipeg's Manitoba Legislative Building.

To this day, bison embody the strength and spirit of the American West. Their image can be found on many important objects. In Canada, the flag of Manitoba province bears the image of a bison, and both the University of Manitoba and the national police force—the Royal Canadian Mounted Police—include bison on their **coats of arms**. The state flag of Wyoming features a white bison, and the state seal of Indiana shows a bison leaping over a log to indicate that bison are still part of a developing landscape. Wyoming, Kansas, and Oklahoma designate the bison as their state animal.

Bison have adorned American money and stamps since the early 20th century. A $10 bill from 1901 featured the image of a bison, and bison have appeared on four postage stamps: the 6-cent, 21-cent, 22-cent, and 30-cent. One of the most famous coins, nicknamed the "buffalo nickel," was produced from 1913 to 1938. The front of the coin bore the head of an American Indian, while on the back was a bison. Its designer, James Earle Fraser, said that he chose these two images because he wanted to create a coin that was distinctly American. In 2005, the U.S. Mint issued a nickel in

Buffalo nickels were issued every year during their 26-year run except in 1922, 1932, and 1933.

Rare white bison are considered to be signs of great spiritual importance to many American Indian tribes.

tribute to the buffalo nickel; its front features Thomas Jefferson, and its back shows a bison. Bison also figure into a series of coins commemorating all 50 states. On the back of the 2005 Kansas quarter is a bison and the state flower, the sunflower. Two bison stand out against the landscape of Theodore Roosevelt State Park on the back of the 2006 North Dakota quarter.

Visitors to Jamestown, North Dakota, can see what is billed as "the world's largest buffalo." It is a steel-and-concrete sculpture created by local artist Elmer P. Peterson that stands 26 feet (7.9 m) tall and 46 feet (14 m) long. In Colorado and Wyoming, many bison artifacts are on display at two famous museums dedicated to one of America's great Western heroes, Buffalo Bill Cody, who was nicknamed "Buffalo Bill" for his hunting skills. The Buffalo Bill Museum & Grave in Golden, Colorado, contains artifacts from Cody's Wild West Show, and the Buffalo Bill Historical Center in Cody, Wyoming, features five museums of the Old West—plus a view of live bison in nearby Yellowstone National Park.

The once thundering herds of bison created an image of strength and speed that people still respect. It's no wonder that numerous sports teams have adopted the bison as their symbol. The National Football League's Buffalo Bills and the National Hockey League's Buffalo Sabres (of Buffalo, New York) both feature the bison prominently in their logos. One of the best-known western colleges, the University of Colorado at Boulder, keeps a live bison named Ralphie as its mascot. Teams at North Dakota State University in Fargo are known as the Bison and nicknamed the "Thundering Herd"; fittingly, their bison mascot is named Thundar.

Although bison have been **domesticated**, they are not easy to train, which is probably why they rarely appear on television or in movies. Perhaps the most famous appearance of bison was in the 1990 film *Dances with Wolves*, in which a private herd of 3,500 bison was rented for use in scenes depicting a buffalo hunt. Two trained bison, Mammoth and Cody, appeared on their own in special scenes. In one, Cody was to chase a young boy. This would have been a dangerous scene to shoot if not for the one item that Cody would perform perfectly to get: Oreo® cookies. Cody was bribed into good behavior by a cookie held behind the camera.

Experts at the National Bison Association estimate that only 1 in every 10 million bison births results in a white bison.

Bison figures appear in ancient petroglyphs, or rock carvings, such as this one on Newspaper Rock in Utah.

REBUILDING THE GREAT HERDS

About 20 million years ago, the first bovid ancestors evolved in Asia. They were part of a growing group of hoofed, grass-eating animals that slowly made their way north. During one of Earth's ice ages, about 300,000 years ago, the first true bison relative, *Bison priscus*, or the steppe wisent, crossed the Bering **Land Bridge** from Siberia into North America. This animal flourished and spread across the continent from Canada to Mexico, but predatory animals—early lions and wolves—followed *Bison priscus*, forcing it to change into a larger, faster animal. (In Europe, *Bison priscus* was replaced by ancestors of the wisent.)

The new species that emerged in North America was *Bison latifrons*. It had horns that measured almost seven feet (2.1 m) across, which it used to defend itself against predators. It lasted until about 22,000 years ago, when changes in land formations and ice barriers led to the evolution of *Bison antiquus*, a species that closely resembled modern bison—except that it was about 20 percent larger.

Wealthier Europeans valued bison as unique animals for hundreds of years, but continual hunting by the

Bison meat has a rich, beef-like taste, but it has 60 to 80 percent less fat and 30 percent fewer calories than beef does.

Visitors to Deadwood, South Dakota, can see a bronze sculpture of 14 bison being driven over a cliff by Indians on horseback.

lower classes—people in need of food—led to the species' serious decline in that part of the world. In 1538, a document issued by Polish king Sigismund I instituted the death penalty for anyone caught **poaching** a wisent. Sigismund also constructed a hunting manor in the village of Białowieza. This became the namesake for the whole forest—Białowieza Forest—which the king declared a hunting reserve in 1541 for the protection of wisent. Unfortunately, wisent were hunted to extinction by 1919, but a herd was rebuilt from zoo animals in the 220-square-mile (570 sq km) Białowieza Forest, which can support only about 800 wisent. Conservationists have taken surplus wisent from Białowieza Forest and reintroduced them to areas of Lithuania, Ukraine, and other eastern European countries in attempts to repopulate dwindling herds. Because of these efforts, the wisent was upgraded from endangered to vulnerable status.

Plains bison were once critically endangered as well, with their numbers reduced from an estimated 60 million to just 600 individuals by 1900. In 1902, only 23 bison remained in Yellowstone National Park, a place that bison had inhabited since prehistoric times. That year, several prominent **zoologists**, including William Temple Hornaday of the New York Zoological Park (now the Bronx Zoo), approached the U.S. government about the need to rebuild wild herds of bison. Twenty-one bison from two captive herds were then released into Yellowstone in an effort to reinforce the population.

In 1912, the American Bison Society chose the Black Hills of South Dakota to be the location of one of the first free-ranging bison herds. The following year, the society donated 14 bison to the Wind Cave National Game Preserve, and now, 100 years later, the herd is nearly 450 animals strong. These bison, as well as the 4,000 living in Yellowstone, are the only **genetically** pure bison in existence, as they contain no cattle **DNA**.

Similar to what happened to plains bison, wood bison populations were decimated in Alaska in the 19th century. Today, conservationists hope to reintroduce wood bison into three major areas of Alaska: the Minto Flats State Game Refuge and the Innoko and Yukon Flats National Wildlife Refuges. Biologist Bob Stephenson of the Alaska Department of Fish and Game spearheaded the Wood Bison Restoration Project in the early 1990s but has

Dances with Wolves *star Kevin Costner commissioned the creation of Deadwood's bison sculpture in 1990.*

Researchers have discovered that one-third of all mature bulls have had at least one rib broken in fights with other bulls.

continually met with resistance from lawmakers who fear the bison will bring diseases such as brucellosis, anthrax, and bovine tuberculosis into the refuges. The debate continues, but Stephenson and the many Alaska Native tribal leaders who support the plan are confident that proper herd management can allow healthy wood bison to roam free in Alaska once more.

Managing bison and keeping them healthy is a challenge. Brucellosis is a disease that mainly affects cattle and results in failure to give birth to live calves, but scientists estimate that about half of Yellowstone's bison have also been exposed to the disease. If these bison leave Yellowstone, they could transmit the disease to domestic cattle on nearby rangeland. The risk of Yellowstone bison transmitting brucellosis to nearby livestock is very low, but cattle ranchers argue that they cannot afford to take chances. Therefore, if bison leave the confines of Yellowstone, ranchers are allowed to shoot them.

Genetic variability, which has to do with the number of differences among individuals in a population of animals, is another important aspect of bison management. Genetic variability in a herd of bison is vital because,

Bison kept in parks are rounded up annually to be counted, branded, and vaccinated against various diseases.

without variability, the herd may not be able to adapt to environmental changes—a weakness that could ultimately lead to **extinction**. Ordway Prairie Preserve in South Dakota is the site of a long-term bison research project, begun in 2003, that studies genetic variability in plains bison.

The research involves how bulls bellow to establish dominance and how an individual's behavior changes as the number of breeding bulls increases in a herd year after year. Researchers led by biology professor Jon Grinnell of Minnesota's Gustavus Adolphus College observe such behaviors as tending, mating, and vocalization to learn

Bellowing indicates aggression and may be followed by a bull stamping his feet, uprooting small trees, and even charging an intruder.

about the messages being sent when bulls bellow. The goal of the research is to find out whether breeding success is determined by herd characteristics or individual behaviors and if smaller herds are capable of breeding with as much genetic variability as larger herds.

Today, 200,000 to 400,000 bison are raised on nearly 5,000 private ranches and farms in the U.S., providing what scientists have found to be one of the healthiest red meats in the world. Most bison are free-ranging and grass-fed, and their meat is free of chemical **hormones** and **antibiotics**—substances which have, in recent years, become objects of concern for consumers of beef, pork, and poultry.

Bison are a valuable part of Earth's prairie wilderness areas, helping maintain the natural balance of their habitats by preventing overgrowth of grassland and providing food for large predators. They also offer cultural, educational, and economic value to humans. It is important for people who share these western environments to respect and manage both human and wildlife activities in order to maintain healthy habitats and populations of wildlife—especially when it comes to the noble bison.

Dried bison droppings, which are often called buffalo chips, were an important source of fuel during the 1800s.

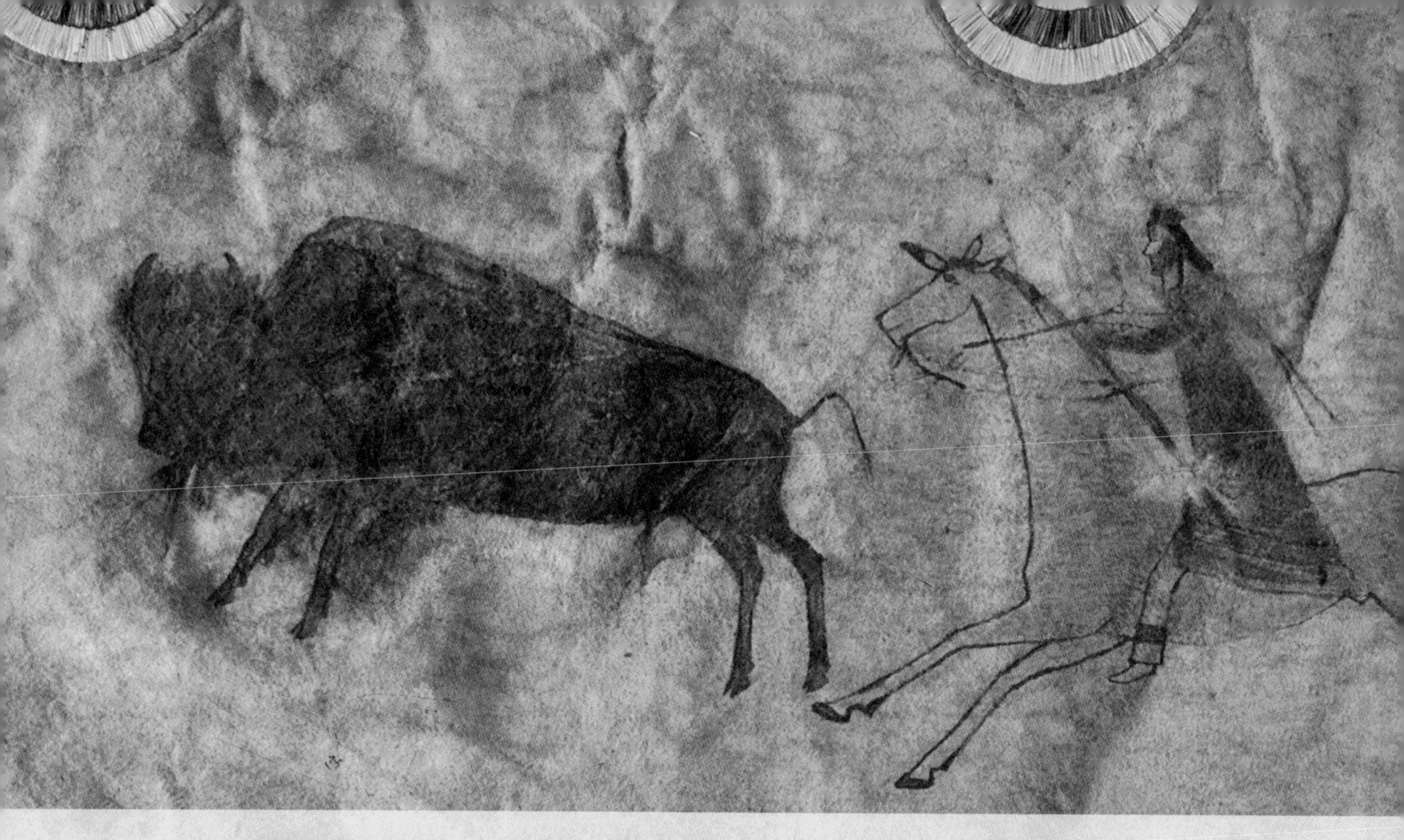

ANIMAL TALE: THE SACRED BISON STONE

The American bison was involved in nearly every aspect of the lives of the native peoples of the North American Great Plains. This story from the Blackfeet Indians, who call bison *iiniiwa*, tells of the sacred bison stone, or *Iniskim*, which is traditionally used in a ritual for calling bison to a hunt.

Long ago, before they had horses, the people hunted bison by driving them off cliffs. But one day, the bison disappeared, and no one knew why. The people began to starve, and their clothes and blankets began to fall apart. Among the people was an old woman. One day while gathering firewood along the trail used to drive bison off the cliffs, the old woman heard someone singing. She discovered the song was coming from a small stone lying in the center of the trail. As she studied the stone, it suddenly cried out to her, "Take me! I am powerful." The woman picked up the stone and held it to her ear, listening as it spoke to her.

When she returned to her camp, she told her husband of her experience. "The stone taught me a song that will bring the bison back," she said. "But the stone says that first you must get me a piece of bison hide from the medicine man."

"How is this possible?" the old woman's husband asked her, looking curiously at the stone in her hand.

"Does it matter?" she replied. "Just get the bison hide." And so the husband did as he was asked and brought his wife a piece of bison hide from the medicine man.

"Next, we must arrange our lodge in a certain way with some sagebrush and bison

chips," the old woman told her husband. He helped her arrange the lodge just as the stone had directed her.

"Now we must ask the men to come and bring their ceremonial rattles," the old woman said. Her husband went out of the lodge and gathered the men, telling them to bring their ceremonial rattles.

The men came, and everyone took seats where the old woman told them to sit. Then the bison stone began to sing, "The bison will return. The bison will return."

As the stone sang its song, the old woman told one of the younger men to take a handful of bison chips to the bison trail. "Put them in a line on the path," she directed. The young man hurried away. The old woman turned to the other men and said, "You must shake your ceremonial rattles and sing along with the stone."

The men began shaking their rattles and singing along with the stone, "The bison will return. The bison will return."

"Sing louder," commanded the old woman. "Shout your song!"

The men sang louder, shouting their song. Soon the young man who had left with the bison chips returned to the lodge, out of breath from running. The stone went silent. The men stopped singing. "The bison chips turned into bison!" the young man told everyone. "And then they ran over the cliff!"

"You see," the stone said, "I am powerful." And from that day on, the people treasured the *Iniskim*, the sacred bison stone, which made the bison plentiful.

GLOSSARY

antibiotics - medicines that kill or disable the growth of bacteria, or living organisms that cannot be seen except under a microscope

archaeologists - people who study human history by examining ancient peoples and their artifacts

coats of arms - the official symbols of a family, state, nation, or other group

DNA - deoxyribonucleic acid; a substance found in every living thing that determines the species and individual characteristics of that thing

domesticated - tamed to be kept as a pet or used as a work animal

evolved - gradually developed into a new form

extinction - the act or process of becoming extinct; coming to an end or dying out

fluctuates - rises and falls in an irregular number or amount

food chains - systems in nature in which living things are dependent on each other for food

genetically - relating to genes, the basic physical units of heredity

gestation - the period of time it takes a baby to develop inside its mother's womb

hormones - chemical substances produced in the body that control and regulate the activity of certain cells and organs

insulating - protecting from the loss of heat

land bridge - a piece of land connecting two landmasses that allowed people and animals to pass from one place to another

lichens - plant-like living things made up of fungus and algae growing in partnership

poaching - hunting protected species of wild animals, even though doing so is against the law

zoologists - people who study animals and their lives

SELECTED BIBLIOGRAPHY

American Bison Society. "Homepage." Wildlife Conservation Society. http://www.americanbisonsocietyonline.org.

American West. "Critters of the West: The American Buffalo." National Bison Association. http://www.americanwest.com/critters/buffindx.htm.

Callenbach, Ernest. *Bring Back the Buffalo!: A Sustainable Future for America's Great Plains.* Berkeley: University of California Press, 2007.

Lott, Dale F. *American Bison: A Natural History.* Berkeley: University of California Press, 2003.

Olson, Wes. *Portraits of the Bison: An Illustrated Guide to Bison Society.* Edmonton: University of Alberta Press, 2005.

Rinella, Steven. *American Buffalo: In Search of a Lost Icon.* New York: Spiegel & Grau, 2008.

Plains bison in Colorado can sometimes be seen roaming the shady pine forests of the Rocky Mountains.

INDEX

Bering Land Bridge 37

bison meat 37, 43

Bovidae family 11, 12

buffalo chips 43

bulls and cows 17, 21, 24–25, 26

calves 25–26
- activities 25, 26
- birth 25
- physical characteristics 25, 26

conservation measures 38, 39–40
- Białowieza Forest 38
- Wind Cave National Game Preserve 39
- Wood Bison Restoration Project 39–40

cultural influences 29–31, 33–35, 38, 43, 44
- artifacts 34
- buffalo nickels and coins 33–34
- coats of arms 33
- film 35
- flags 33
- modern art forms 34, 38
- on native North Americans 29–31, 44
- sports mascots 35
- symbolic importance 30, 34

dangers 29, 30–31, 37–38, 40
- diseases 40
- hunting by humans 29, 30–31, 37–38
- poaching 38

domestication 35

European bison *see* wisent

feeding 7, 18, 21, 22, 23
- and digestion 18
- plant sources 18, 21, 22, 23
- and water consumption 21

Grinnell, Jon 41

habitats 7–8, 11, 18, 22, 23, 24, 25, 29, 37, 38, 39, 40, 43
- Europe 11, 38
- and food chains 22, 43
- forests 23, 38
- North America 7, 11, 29, 37, 39, 40
  - Canada 11, 29
  - United States 7, 11, 29, 39, 40
- plains and prairies 7–8, 18, 23, 24, 25, 29

Hornaday, William Temple 39

life expectancy 24

mating 24–25, 40, 41
- male competition 25, 40

movement 17, 21, 24
- on land 17, 21, 24
- swimming 21

parent-child relationship 26

physical characteristics 8, 12, 15, 17, 18, 24, 25, 30, 37
- fur 8, 15, 18, 30
- guard hairs 15
- heads 18, 25
- hooves 18, 24, 30
- horns 12, 18, 24, 25, 37
- humps 15
- legs 24
- senses 17
- sizes 15, 17
- tails 17

plains bison 10, 11, 15, 17, 21, 23, 24, 38, 39

populations 12, 17, 21, 29, 38, 39, 40–41, 43
- genetic variability within 40–41, 43
- relocation of 21, 38, 39

predators 23–24, 25, 26, 37, 43
- bears 24
- wolves 23, 24

relatives 11, 12, 37
- ancestors 11, 37
- bovids 11, 37

scientific research 41, 43
- Ordway Prairie Preserve 41

social behaviors 7, 21, 23, 24, 26, 41, 43
- living in bands or herds 7, 21, 23, 24, 26, 43
- vocal communication 21, 41

Stephenson, Bob 39

white bison 33, 34

wintering grounds 23, 24

wisent 10, 11, 12, 26, 37, 38

wood bison 10, 11, 15, 17, 23, 39–40
- and reintroduction efforts 39